To write is to ascend downward, as Hélène Cixous says, and it's this downward ascension that James Pate writes in *Mineral Planet* where "roots spread upwards / through ribcage and skies." Reading, then, becomes a kind of digging that's not an excavation so much as an attendance to what's left behind: sequins, wet depths, wallpaper, barbed wire, sunlight in ice. Nearly imperceptible glimmers become planets we orbit as *Mineral Planet* descends to reveal slivers of "Saints with meatlaced faces" and the "flesh of our thoughts." Transcendence becomes an unrelenting participation in what's fleeting: "Several all at once, and then none, ever again."

Emmalea Russo, Author of *Wave Archive* and *Confetti*

Costumes of feather and flesh, the hissing of angels – in this texture-drunk into the matter and mineral of life, James Pate perverts US literary culture's demand for narrativity, selfhood, order, with a poetry so gorgeously atmospheric even language itself becomes onyx. The saints of this baroque vision are artists – Iggy Pop, Fassbinder, St Teresa – because artists, especially artists who dare to go all the way, understand that gold is an ornament. It's worthless.

Johannes Göransson, Author of *The Sugar Book* and *Summer*

Like plunging one's entire head into a black mirror, *Mineral Planet* offers glimpses of a desolate future in which our legacy as human beings is merely a persistent afterimage burned onto the surface of reality. *Mineral Planet* reads as a leaky, spliced film created by a wistful collector: reader-viewers only witness glimpses and fragments of human landscapes and ruin, but each vision is lovingly curated. Visually saturated and highly sensory, Pate offers disarming Gothic pleasure in utter annihilation.

M. Forajter, Author of *Interrogating the Eye*

With its drifting, staccato decay, James Pate's Mineral Planet presents us with a litany of impersonal affects, strewn with the flourishing desiderata of an already-dead planet, manic in its transcendental decline.

Eugene Thacker, Author of *Infinite Resignation*

"Behind the nothing stirring stirred everything." Much like "Sister Midnight" – the David Bowie/Iggy Pop song that slithers its way through James Pate's brilliant *Mineral Planet* – these vibrant, meat-slick poems mask something teeming and unpolished. These are poems in infinite process, language fragments that reconcile the wind-swept remnants of fires, silicates, and keratins with raw human experience. From the smallest cells to the farthest, darkest stars, *Mineral Planet* is utterly alive and always becoming – a "planet of remembrance and abhorrence" – like so many dragonflies to sew you up.

David Peak, Author of *Corpsepaint* and *The Spectacle of the Void*

James Pate's *Mineral Planet* is so many haute pleasures all at once: it's a consideration of "symbols without stories" (maybe even obliquely referencing a filmmaker's work on a 2009 advertisement for investment company Allan Gray in which appears James Dean's iconic face cleanly edited into a different reality, one in which he lives to be old); it's a study in mashing together overt and covert allusions to create an absolutely succulent world–like as if Joe Gillis of *Sunset Boulevard* were floating dead and facedown in Norma Desmond's pool but staring at an Iggy Pop poster at the bottom; it's a call, via decadent but aloof partying and the cinematic gaze, for "kaleidoscopic Bosch-ian communism"; it's about funeral-theater and miming and apocalyptic luxury and maybe the velvet, vampy David Lynch feeling of the 90s; it's "gardens where the nothing happening happens" and "nightflood spillage," possibly in service of embracing Plato's indictment of poets in that the book really laps up of the "honey poison" of its own tastes.

It gave me the sensation of a single scene in a Polish film the title of which I've never been able to remember: partygoers wander into an amusement park in the middle of the night, and they drunkenly turn on the rides and end up falling asleep in those carnival swings high up in the air. It's upsetting and wonderful. I love their outfits and smeared makeup, and my pleasure in this possibly corroded memory finds kinship with Pate's "bird-shit windowsills," "infinite metallic symphonies," "colors of moldy Polaroids," and – get this! – archaic names for wigs!

Olivia Cronk, Author of *Skin Horse* and *Womonster*

MINERAL
PLANET

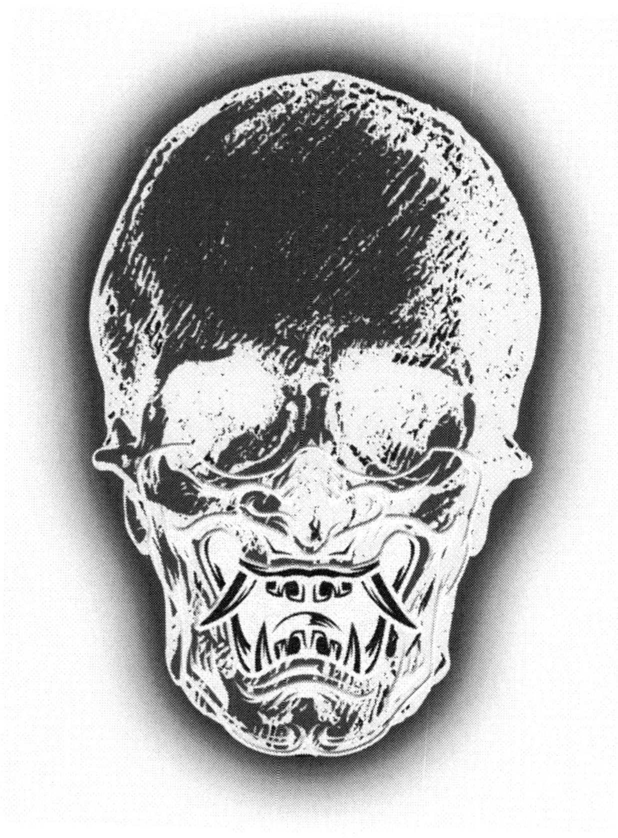

First published in 2022 by

Schism Nεuronics

First edition
ISBN: 9798841380283

Cover design by GJS

Printed in London, UK.

MINERAL
PLANET

James Pate

Ash, Onyx, & Feather

From up there there was no smoke to see / gray thread curling up from bright charcoals where the eyes once shifted / how I heard one game ending in the next room / another one lighting its matches among the garlands and urns in the den / ashdrips from the seams of the windows /

Throats painted with fingertip blood / I heard what they said from the floorboards /

A balcony from which the vinyl ones wrestled and descended / honeydrip wings latched into the blades of each shoulder / snug and sewn hard /

Crimson vinyl tight on every inch / a tongue wet from cold blue milk / leashes of garland from baluster to baluster, joint to corroded joint /

From the horizon, roads digging into the forest / its stitched and threaded fires / through this long falling upwards and over

The game neither older nor newer, the sky neither colder nor warmer / the fronds part memory and part landscape / figures with mineral mouths chewing, muttering / they told me of their practices and eradicating codes /

A number channel on the radio folded into a blank summer day / edges torn with light / an hour in July behind the diner, framed by an autochrome sky /

I heard the angels hissing / I felt the spider in their spider corners / laptop screen fastened to the northern wall, lava glittering forth /

Underneath and all around / caves of hot fog, breastbones of saturated fur /

Mineral planet, ash planet, planet with glowing charcoal eyes, planet of remembrance and abhorrence / planet of star and seed / poison and petal / eye and echo /

A tunnel from which an amphitheater emerged, pink in the crestfallen light / a dying sun among newborn stars / languages of onyx and rosewater /

I crouch by the tree, I dip my hands into the reflection of the branches / a chemical pond shimmering in the carbonized heat /

Nothing ever heard there nor found / skies encased in skies under our feet / nothing slipping underneath and through where the cheek joined briefly with jaw

Arms among the branches pointed downwards into earth, fingers flexing / letting go / red moon wide as the sun / bitegrips in the palms of each spent hand /

I ride out to the stone tower / the bird-shit windowsills / ruins of a picnic in the front lawn / porcelain angels with outstretched faces / rust in the curvatures between wing and spine / storms over the eastern mountain gathering their satin drapery /

Little remains, or was meant to /

Wickerchair weeds /

Cherubs stare from this ceiling, their thoughts with no core, only passages and corridors / I am their insect, their breathing bird / ceremonial figures walking with bared feet over filthy carpets / plush vine patterns /

Sister Midnight, I pray like a pierced mask / Homer's arrow in our throats, oddshaped meats crackling over bonfires / our cups gathering drifting ash / flakes from the dark overhead / night latched snug with latex stars /

Sister Midnight, your red meadow-glow /

Several all at once, and then none, ever again /

It was over before it had started / this ruin, taken further / curdled milk, mossy jaws, translucent bellies / a million melting edifices along the reflective waterscape / the hum in the clean café, the two of them across the table /

Shores of pink sugar light /

Raw expressions in the bark they pass by /

The snow-stitched beach / frostbreath seeping in / dusk extinguishing the rooms from basement to attic / night enfolding the trees / traffic lights dangling over blank roads /

Off the lakeshore the couple blended / web-worked and extricated / shoulders and calves and stillness and not-stillness / dunes of grit and glitter in their steady unmaking /

Then dressing in black wet garments / sniffing their more intimate drugs /

Remnants of themselves left behind / sickly sweet corruption /

Curled, mossy, unbleached, unmoored /

This film decades ago / an emerald storm / clouds with their human features unwinding, dissolving / lightning from below not above /

In the garden of gray latex foliage / moths spinning about, chewing through / trembling hands in front of the broken, seeping masks / a static emerald memory lodged in the back, reflecting the partylights / the bulb at the end of the hall at the end of the feast blinking in the graydawn light /

Lovesick sweet cannibalism /

We drank the wine in the den, among the mounted heads and depthless glass irises / a glitching river of lava current beneath the oceans underneath us / shaven figures struggling among themselves, biting through the middles /

Nightflood spillage / in glass pupils /

Silent morning / long windows / coffee and grapes and butter / hours of heresy / blood from eyes and mouths and ears / statues with meaty edible hearts / vestibules brimming with pink gelatinous light /

Downfacing Attic Plays / singular pain with hundreds of mouths parting /

The highest sibilant register/ clouds high below us / never a now but a many /

Sister Midnight, Queen Midnight, Red Midnight, Red Queen, Carrion Queen, Attic Queen, Sister Twin, Sister Dusk, Sister Eclipse, Sister Arson, Sister Nero, Queen Red, Queen Blank, Queen Tremor, Sister of the Velvet Basements, Queen of the Back-broken Chairs, Queen of the Rabid Statuary, Sister of Fortune, Sister of Grace, Sister of Obscurer Elements, Sister of Cloud and Fire, Queen Serpent, Queen of the Meatlace Sky, Queen Mourning, Sister of the Rosyfingered Dusk, Sister of Glittering Startrash, Sister Morning:

Saints with meatlaced faces / crows in their bellies / rubber dayglo rib bones /

I've been hearing them / interiority in the hazed distance / words with their directions carved out / eyes flat as dripping stone / sludge in the undertow /

Angels from which no names will emerge / heads without faces / a summer hour no one recalls / the curling and colliding in that room, folding into and out of the others, lips and breath and ankle / backwards and backlit /

Games of ash and angelsong, parlors of spilled ruby tea / snakeskin walls /

Enough forgetfulness to lose some and countless more /

Out of which this statue shines / arms missing / hands alert / eyes scratched out and mouth shifting, muttering / a heavenly tongue flashing, forked /

Red Velvet Choirs

Beach breeze through their hair / the beach hum of traffic / hands of evening in their fingers, along their stomachs / a night spent in Hawk Garden / swans in their costumes of feather and flesh /

Someone will emerge through these pewter symphonies / speak of lunches nestled near violent seas / others will join us on the terrace / flesh of our thoughts among the flesh of those vines / theologies of great sweat and disbelief / snakes will coil around our scarlet organs / tigers will climb from perches / devour us with perfect jaws / infinite metallic symphonies / long warm throats / the music playing elsewhere /

Sister Midnight, we've waited this long in birth / Sister Midnight, your hallways are high and icy / your beach is not ours /

Bright, wordless nights / an endless serpentine unworlding /

Sister Midnight, this ballad of snow and coats with furred collars / Iggy Pop on the poster in the basement / leatherfaced and stringhaired / mineral-eyed swans at his shoulders /

Long avenues of ash, Sister Midnight, call out your step /

Tease us tighter, up along our eyes / stalks breathing in ripples of night / the cornices holding up these Edens of filthy fingers / hard teeth /

Threads of lavender smoke from vents in the distance /

Beyond the serpentine hedges / past the hotel's Blade Lake /

The first three films of Rainer Werner Fassbinder /

St. Teresa in gold /

Soft noises followed by softer ones /

Extinguishing hot hours, breakfasts we finished on balconies by leaden ponds, the stories the others told us of cold angels with leaflatched wings / beyond the weeds and fronds rustling over the still ones we call sleeping /

Beyond animal vegetable mineral / looping in and through /

Pink steam rising through carbonized branches / the pool drained, shutters closed, the shed ablaze / angels with leafthick features descending /

What they did afterwards upstairs, in basements, the hours they spoke of /

Petals and pink insect shells around the coliseum / bitten pomegranates / a procession silent as breeze through tonguewide fronds /

Paradise of slippage, spoilage /

Unleashed branches erupting downwards from upturned faces /

Heads of fire approaching, a single manic eye in the taut leather terrain / sky teeming with curling ignited bark, unstrung celestial dust / soft bellies alive in the meadow / loosened gray matter dreaming at the roots /

Plato's sun the moon / the scorched inner artery of the cave / exploratory sensations frothing novel glitchworks in our heads / angels frozen in bulbscream /

Out from this everywhere, nowhere / flames lick up, blank holes in the air / burnt rooms in the memoryhive / gardens where the nothing happening happens /

Names covered in moss and moss inscribing names / along the backs of the last ones, the winged ones, unburied ones / with teeth from neverbefore / gnashing, thrashing /

Biting into exposed parts, the breathable curves / soil mixed with fruit seed / acidic weather and outages / vinegary poison rising through / cool flesh /

The crimson light / dusk-sentient vines / blistering each and every off / an inner light already out there, stalking and towering, high with whispers / carrion mist /

The concrete amphitheater dotted with fur ones and emerald ones / the noises in our throats, the impervious Augusts, iron trees with lush deteriorating edges /

Tattoos on their spines of rhizomatic crafting, spills and spells, the eye we pretended to be painted on our skies, witnessing /

Pearls in the onyx ashtray inside the crumblecake lobby, coiled undergrowth below shatterwork marble, careless cloud drift, the methods of rodents with their rodent minds and rodent landscapes / under rodent skies /

Outside echoing in the interior /

Interior pulsing with exterior /

Water reflection and greenish tints under the viaduct /

No admission, no pass, no entryways to thread through, only wandering about, puddles of pink hues past the concrete archways /

The collapsed steel lacework, the last lingering murmurs mammalian and angelic /

Rock formations + storm-cloud formations + crow formations +
beaks pressed high and upward against pink sky /

What dripped down through our throats and out the ends of our hair /
honeyed poison unclenching / releasing /

Flame surrounding each humming stone /

Rain clatter, wind tearing through the leaves: Spring, with its purple froth and orange-eyed eruptions / its webbing caught in silver light / the town faded: a ship coasting on night clouds / insects trilling in wet branches /

I heard nothing, awoke no one / crows loved us and remained by our side / when we opened our chests to them / flame blazed forth /

They smelled along our bones, entered into our night / pines purred with smoke / nighthammer and nightsickle / God's bite marks in our sides /

Spring, with its high-worn violets and soiled mouth and gilded cornice / its bare foot leaving bloodied toe prints / whistling grass /

Born in the hour of insomnia / petals dropping on plates of meat and cartilage /

Sister Midnight, our plateau will crumble first, followed by the mansions we have built upon it /

Sister Midnight, the black cloths you lend us, the forked instruments, the burnt remainders you leave in our lower garden /

Foliage thawing over felines playing Statue /

This was already then, in the other Eternal Evening / before waking in the glittering dawn among polished eyes and sculpted trees /

Sister Midnight, inside your many faces speaks your many tongues /

The countless, the plurality / muddied stomachs breathing bright new air / kaleidoscopic Bosch-ian communism /

So many other days have included such impulses, without us / in the cemetery I buried dried violets / in the Church of Latex, saints with neon eyes /

The windswept, anonymous future /

Sister Midnight, lead us through this radiant avenue / to the lasting bitter fronds /

They touched your cold forehead in the film from which we recognized the others / years ago, on the cold beach /

And once before / and then /

The hands moving out from under us / north, south, east, west / in movies of hard blue light / black unfurling skies /

Guests among the rocks discovering tarnished utensils and leaky fruit / in musty gowns and splattered suits / from one year up towards others, into thinner and glossier light /

The dinner party of dark velvet glances and moths inside the bellies /

Cigarettes smoked upstairs in shredded masks, in frozen ripening poses /

A thousand cold windows to see through / to escape from /

Traveling under the flat-topped mountains / their hips chalked with skulls and lilies / on the train beneath the city / watching ghost faces linger on black glass / nearing midnight / we eat the midnight candy /

Our tongues turn toward fleeting gilt syllables / cold smoke haloing lamps flanking the roads of Overture Park / rain splashes on our leftovers / our arsenic hair and redstitched desires / our fingertip nostalgia / our cooing throats /

Memories of attics and frost and ancient mattresses /

Imprint of my breath on the window / the syntax of ruins and faded tattoos and rooms high above the streets /

Illustrated books of guillotines and grinning throats /

Even the air is illicit / an altar anywhere is belief everywhere /

In the angel factory they remake us nightly / shoulder and joint, breast and midriff, marrow and waist / pressing their whispers and tinfoil feathers into our warm cavities / damp expectant lungs /

And later, small espressos in the vast café, the backs of heads in mirrors / blue wigs and dyed feathers / a wandering Germanic fairytale /

He kneels in front of the other / bare damp skin lit by many windows / rain-soaked shirts on the chair next to their shifting shadows / the light burns through / chandeliers and snowdrip / dead eyes reflecting flames /

Birdshadow circling over the rug, ashes in the weave /

Thinking of the director, the actors / the creatures witnessing from the branches / oceans mentioned in the script / us in the audience / in our balmy clothes / in our muddied hair / the hum of lit spaces / rain cascading in café mirrors / the future shaping us in its faceless image / churches with flashing neon mouths under massive palm trees /

The number of the dead we name / the presider in the pierced mask /

Pink room by the shoreline, its red paintings murmuring /

Clutching on, in the flexing venomlight /

Shore whispers of this red planet /

This ruin and the surrounding soil / sunken stones and green
afternoons / the gowns and tuxes in which they found their drugs /

And after this, and us, the empty, sprawling parking lots / lamps
dimming one by one / red dust fingerprints here and over there /

The parade roamed through, toward the longer shadows and the scent of fires /passed glittering roadkill and shorn doorways /

Past patchwork tents, lungs of black leather inhaling /

Walked under trees with brutalized trunks /

Through hallways of bittertasting shrubs /

The woman by the stream, her eyes dark and seeing / chorus of ironwork angels / calling forth and from out /

How rock calcified into bone and wind into speech / no one threaded in the everyone and elsewhere / a number station counting backwards toward the opening /

A parade of frost-sharp flowers, of gasping fish with staring eyes /

She slit them open, gutted the inedible portions / her masks our masks / her mouth always at our lips / stamped tin, cold gold / crumble-eyed

Dreaming in their bellies / violets and lilies blooming in their nightpockets / in steadfast and imploding descent /

Between cults and religions /

Shadows heighten /

Bioluminescent dreamworks /

The train emerging from the billion city lights /

The robin falling from the branches, thudding like flint at our feet /

He polishes the casket in the yard /

He's five and the weather is static and hot and senseless /

A dog is lost and considered dead /

The robin retreats into greenery /

A dog barks at the soft spots in the yellowing yard /

The casket is lowered /

Wearing the black suit to the pool party /

Burning wicker thrones in the fevermeadow /

As only the body lives on /

A freckle of silver poison on the lip of each plastic leaf /

I entered the room with my one key / placed my garments and watch on the marble table / named my drug / slept in the tepid water of the bath /

In the room above Lou Reed sang of squalor and Berlin / he's dead / songs drifting from someplace where he's dead /

A courtyard of antic pigeons /

A gray figure in pearls watching / an unlit window / smoking the final cigar /

Afterwards, they washed their arms / their backs /

I studied my features / a sudden human mask /

I poured drinks as the party started / its chiffon dress slipping over bare, muddied feet /

Near the end of the millennium / corridors of statuary and cephalopods /

Biographies of luminescent fungi / ornate dinners among the Warhol wigs /

Our walls of tumbling floral wallpaper / our stairwell of yellow night / mineral angels drawing roses on their pelvises / air changing into light, breath into dissonance / the window bloodied from mistaken birds /

The gray man finding his way below us, into waiting basements / smelling of wind and sea-spray / leaving iron-gray hair in our coats /

Narcotic speeches at turquoise parties / funerals at the Gulf, during the balmy trips south / moths dancing around the coffinfeet / statues with underwater eyes /

Flecks of fire emerging from angel tongues /

Without foresight or purpose / into sand shelving towards its tide /

Drifting into one another, among the long-throated pedestals / tableaux of grimacegrin mouths / among trickling fruit /

The wages of those awful days / the glossy crimson door at the curve of the unkempt lane / red veils, gleaming pews / ceiling splattered and fringed with watchful eyes /

Curtains burning in the houses on high /

Nowhere/Elsewhere/Everywhere

Weather a type of thought and thought a type of weather /

Wine and champagne and incense / rotting leaves in corroding gutters / dinner party séance / costume party liturgy /

A look from a leaden window / rain-worn / bones behind floral wallpaper dead as the moon / and as bright /

Between the mask and its eye / between the tongue and air and the word / between serene belief and majestic heresy / between tip of flame and spear of star /

Angels of salt frozen along the shoreline / grain by grain blown
Elsewhere / garbed in moss and desiccated shrubbery / hips without
legs, shoulders without chests /

Unwound, unstrung / holes in the flesh through which the wind
burns /

Through the stony bluff the precession wound / salt breeze chafing /
halo oilflames along the viaduct / high beasts of rust from which ivy
clings /

Heights of each pit, heavens of air in the caverns /

Flakes of cold rust in our eyes / whalebones, snake skins, oily hair / they took him apart, unhinging piece from piece / aftermath in an El Greco horizon / clusters of thorns worn around the waist / bared teeth and torsos /

Wings beating against our cheeks / lavender bleached skies/ rubies, pistols, and weeds /

God continued speaking in many other voices / the figures in tuxedoes thrashing through the bamboo grove / rouge dots on cheeks, foreheads / dead seagulls swaying from balconies / teeth buttons along the back of the black skirt /

Downstairs, a cat wail followed by another /

Animal noise licking up the walls of one another /

The rosary beads the ones with faces would wear to bed / a party far off, tumbling / into lacy sea churn / confetti in the mannequin's curls /

Continually one day nearer / crepes in a cold hotel / mountains of snowing swirling into mountains of water, lit by different shades of night / no one at the counter /

Animalvast / starbroken / ironlace revolutions /

Everyone has always been late / in fur and silk pants / in leather and ink / in flesh and in mind / in films watched and forgotten / in figures cleaned and undone /

The actors were rabbits infected with human nightmares / hotel rooms bright with snowglare / wolves from ancient myths involving lovers and thawing dusk /

Everyone an envelope and those envelopes reversible and they could never read what was written inside because they were always a little outside /

A pool surrounded by shrub trees the color of chemical stains /

Lit candles, burning among tree crowns / curvatures of stars with every ground giving way / the card revealing the beheaded pelican floating on the skylit surface /

Rabbits with their human-mouthed nightmares / in the pool-house, the body unmoved and unmoving / behind the nothing stirring stirred everything /

This near Chicago / the gathering moved in grey coats, shivering / their backs lit by arson / ceremonies and lingering fevers / lice living deep down /

The spine of some inner chord shifting / a metallic music played, as if we lived with silver hair among polished shoes /

Sleep swirled above us, between our minds and the ceiling / a certain afternoon light never leaves / faces of No One / in clouds, among the tree barks / in some last museum in frigid unlit air /

November with its perverse purples / colors of moldy Polaroids / in the distance, and several years before / bonfire feasts / sprigs of cilantro in synthetic hair / perukes damp in the tides / whitehaired seaweed / tumbling into and scratching out of /

Smoky silhouettes with teeth and nervous tongue /

Waves of acid green /

Electric violet silences /

Beaches sprawling out in blinking light /

Damp fishy clumps peeling apart in our fingers /

Faces of scraped salt / their not-eyes / the ones buried in us / tucked in livid flesh /

Afterwards, Allan Gray in a pool in southern California /
An emptied hotel with empty windows /
In some versions he's the dead man's float /
In others he's on his back, adrift in the square of green water /
On top a pink and dotted inflatable /
Misty air and trickling trees /
Ringed by oiled foreheads of fire /
Sunlight hard and high and casting no shadow /
Leone combing her hair in the canvas chair /
Rooms of dust and orange carpets with occult stains /
A single red spider in the drain /
Around the pool, the remainder of the state /
The rest of what some people call California /
Mountains on a planet /
Carl Dreyer's *Vampyre* playing in a room inside a million other rooms /
Low buildings on long streets /
Trees around, dead in the living light /
Leone humming a song from the other place /
A film curling with shadow /
Her sister-self turning toward the camera /
Allan with his long corpse features and live corpse eyes /
His family having passed into that light leaving him nothing /
Except here /
This smell of chemicalized water /
The green slime corpse life of water /
On which he floats /
In some scenes dead and in others dead and staring /

Extended games stumbling feralwise into the edge of the interlacing branches /

Silent mineral oceans / the little land we knew and lived on / angels of roving choir light below us, above /

Molting feathers / molten rock / streams of bird cries from leather mouths / powder and rouge to mask the fever / sweat dripping / melting clean scars into their cheeks /

Startrash Picnic

Silence in the streets, inside the automobiles / only fingers and lips twitching / the countless manners in which living turns live /

November light ruffling dark through elms / stone birdbaths / a few last partygoers in motely burnt clothes in the windows of Shadow House / bright lit panes, specks of snow drifting on frozen marble tongues /

Skinshedding hours /

Rippling upwards downwards the ghostflesh /

Spiritgasped /

We lived in basements and attics / growing hair and shaving hair / cutting toenails in quiet, secluded corners /

Dog barking from out the human throat, angel grimacing through the human mouth /

Wide windows in the hotel lobby / dripping garlands woven through chipped balustrade / leatherbound doors / leaves drifting from cracked corners / crosshatched Guest List /

Stretched and soundless mirror glances /

Forms of burnt meat / opaque breathing materials /

Sister Midnight in our hands and through our eyes / planetlight staring through us / touching around us / hard and brittle bones / an almost-music in those lungwet depths / leftover sequins on bare throats / newer glittering nights /

Because every hour stares at twilight /
Because the hands and thighs of this late hour /
Because these voices /
Because these hanging mouths of air /
Because the dead never visit their own cemeteries /
Because cloudshadow moves over their features /
Because a number of the living lives among us /
Because of bewitched mineral hunger /
Because of no reason and never a reason, without end /
Because bodies exist in weather /
Because hair grows in graves /
Because what is is already tumbling beneath us /
Because of bloodied grass and wrestling thorns /
Because gloves are masks for fingers /
Because of the moths and angels eating through /
Because of theologies of eccentric flesh /
Because the cold shoulder of art /
Because ruins become us /

Symbols without stories /

Meadows without maps /

Clouds in the cheval mirror /

To be emptied out, the self always behind our heads /

An ashtray filled with pearls, parlor game veils, silent storm hours /

Lavaside swelling, heavenswift stuckage /

Until and beyond / an extinguished cigarillo, moldy cake, floral arsenic wallpaper / the anonymous postcard on the last desk in the finalized corridor /

Tuesdays of velvet masked attendees /

Cosmology where naming erodes the thing named / turns it toward us /

Fields of cloth black flowers in autochrome colors / wormwood growing, spilling around ankles and ears / trampling through, hip-high / smokestacks never growing nearer in the frosted distance / a long dead spring morning from which they and we emerged / frothing, dripping, petaling / makeshift rituals encrusted with jewels and barbed-wire / shorn and feathered and reborn /

Between the blue era of soil / the violet era of silk / plague parks / Shroud Palace /

Air from which the mouths bled through / the Fassbinder ending where a single lit cigarette concludes the proceedings /

Roots spreading upwards / through ribcages and skies /

Marketwatch and the police it guides into our heads /

Under a palm tree with his dead eyes staring /
Upwards, a plain of arid blue /
Breeze stirring fronds and the hems of his clothes /
Allan Gray infected with film light /
Multiplied by film shadow /
A name being a symbol that bleeds through /
Past face, hair, and skull /
Crackling soundtrack, rooms of old film scratches /
Intertitles blurred, syntax corroding /
Flat fields of flat trembling angels /
Carnal metaphors for spectral hungers /
All else lit from within / cracks of sunlight in ice /

Drinking from a tiny blue cup in a vacant café / to live here / among these shapes and sights, to breathe near the edge of this river curving towards increasing night / a child at a pool party holding out an orange / the crimson nose of a deceased dog floating past / hills like sleeping muscle in the pink fog / leafnetted and root pierced /

At the edge of the river black duck feathers brushed by wind, the
stillness beneath the feathers rotting into a curled renegade shape /
boats sped into tunnels of trees / four
in the afternoon / angels with veined halos on fire in the trees /
lovely rising smoke / beyond scent and sight / luxuriant alienages /
spidereye, birdeye, leafeye /

Bodies through which other bodies emerge /

Lycanthropy in Petronius / among stonebulks in brisk dusk /

Late days trembling blue /

Tub water blushing / bathing live and emerging dead /

Sister Midnight, her Shadow Monuments with blazing crowns /

Sister Midnight of the scorched trunks and leaf /

Sister Midnight of 4 am dance clubs, morningdusk, our steadfast
twilights /

Wreathed in ivy, the dead face sinking inward, rusting holes whistling / December forms of lavender and hemlock / mint thickening out from torn cheeks / latex kisses / muscle prints in the dusk-snow / morning wine, evening coffee / teeth red from cake / the airy distances / whistling through, whistling in / writhing solstice figures and forms / night treks along the frolicking, wavering edge /

Figures in smudged costume tumbling into one then tumbling out as many /

Bouts of Ravenous Pierrot /

Ornamented pits /

A cold perpetual hunger /

Bodies without heads, throats without necks /

Winter lights threaded through the carrion field /

Our threadbare festivities /

Angular dancing in the misted courtyard air /

Jumping / fingering / thrashing /

Shapeshifting musculature and dripping glitterbeads /

How face becomes memory then cloud /

Whatevers and whoevers watching through our eyes /

Frequencies we pretend to own /

Elements enfolded in elements, in long rain, in seeping woodland ciphers /

Shoulders and hips of grime

Swaying in the Last Moon nights / not a tongue

Not a dustspeck

Shifting /

Tides stilled, feathers patchworked among dunes /

Only a leaden, headless dance, throats nude and glistening

In clubs without music or stage /

Sister Midnight, the festival drifts basementward, the Pierrot masks congealing / tightening into / this lifting silver pain who has become our Host /

Sister Midnight, the vaporous ones you wander among / occulted engineering /

Late night coffee in late night diners /

Angels in their last feathering /

Vinegar smell of their mouths / cold tinsel stars falling through our outer spaces /

Film of beach scenes / mossgreen picnic / glittery torsos / playing / a clip too fast / fingers wine-red in the cold / mouthshapes muttering sweet nothings / numbed anonymous poses / interlocking and echoic and mercurial /

Shadowcoves / scarlet chemtrails under planetsized moons /

Tendrils from Before / outspills of After / under skies of marble and ice / weeds our brains grow into /

April with its skittering rainlight / fringe of glossy fronds around the casket in the den, children in twitchy clothes and twitching limbs gathering / looking in /

Underworlds underneath with their damp curving acreages / from which other voices hiss of far-flung minds / Enkidu in the house of dust / April froth from our throats /

Falcons gathering around the den / paper human-masks with mouths but no eyes / shivering, extracting / bright-dark mineral bones calcifying / rocks and jawline waterfalls

Glass made in heaven by angels with one red dot on each wing / honeygolden shoulders, as shown in the finer magazines of that era / lampshades strewn by the breeze / along the sweep of river / stone cornices eyeing, unclosing/ scenes of glitchdance and sliced mansions / curtains damp in the branches / wine spilling along the cliffside / falcons plummeting upwards / blue wings against blue air /

The banquet with its dribbling champagne, its midnight crepes, cocaine conjurings / trailing muddied furs / withdrew through the morning air of the terrace /

One by singular one /

Dirty plates in the bathtub, counters of unfinished meats / birds pecking among /

I was in the pool, floating like a child dazed by the glare of his birthday /

In the hills, a procession / in the haze-distance / morningstruck, numbstruck / hollowedeyed / further from, not out /

Light streamed from the wounds / downwards / caverns in our thoughts and underfoot / no core, only labyrinths / pomegranate stigmata /

A veiled and carnal mourning / feet of ivy, scalp of smoke / conversing with the dead ones inside us / the eyes in us they wake from /

Acknowledgements

Thank you to the following journals, which published poems from *Mineral Planet*. (The original poems have sometimes been altered for this collection.)

Occulum: [Sister Midnight, Queen Midnight, Red Midnight], [Beach breeze through their hair], and [Sister Midnight, we've waited this long in birth]

Burning House Press: [The concrete amphitheater] and [Symbols without stories]

Spoon River Poetry Review: [Near the end of the millennium], [Sister Midnight, our plateau will crumble first], and [Sister Midnight, inside your many faces speaks your many tongues]

Heavy Feather Review: [In the garden of gray latex foliage], [The parade roamed through, toward the longer shadows], and [Angels of salt frozen along the shoreline]

Also available from SCHISM NEURONICS

Interrogating the Eye – M. Forajter
The Selected Poems of Charles Tomás – translated by Carlos Lara and Tamas Panitz
Book of Losses – Joseph Turrent
KRV – Oli Johns
Sorcererer – Jace Brittain
Sonnet Cycle – Tom Will
Burton's Anatomy – Ansgar Allen
The Fall Garment – Paul Cunningham
The Isotope of I – Connor Fisher
The Reading Room – Ansgar Allen
You Alive Home Yet? – Daniel Beauregard
The Reaches – Ansgar Allen
> Get Back to Work – Jim Redmond
Everjescence – Tyson Bley
Work is Hard Vore – Philip Sorenson
Vagabond – Joshua Martin
The –Tempered Mid·Riff – Brad Baumgartner
I Get Groceries – RC Miller
Lynx Perpetual Lynx – Colin Post
Wretch – Ansgar Allen
A Large Retailer – RC Miller
Spelunker – Mike Corrao
Gynophobia – Tyson Bley
Normal Service Will Resume Shortly – Tyson Bley
Cyclops – Tyson Bley
Demon Drawings – RC Miller
Dark Poems – Tyson Bley
Frankencop – Tyson Bley
Celestial Chimp – Tyson Bley

Also available from SCHISM^2

Subconscious Colossus – Carlos Lara
Slow Hot – Andy Choi
Snuff Memories – David Roden
An Ideal For Living – Eugene Thacker
The Autobiography of Leisure – Narco Pastel
The House of the Tree of Sores – Paul Cunningham
Left Hand – Paul Curran
Coma Crossing: Collected Poems – Roger Gilbert-Lecomte, translated by David Ball
A Slow Boiling Beach – Rauan Klassnik
Serial Kitsch – Gary J. Shipley
Sacer – Nicola Masciandaro
Amygdalatropolis – B. R. Yeager
All the Messiahs – Anonymous
Thank You, Steel China – Sean Kilpatrick
Crypt(o)spasm – Gary J. Shipley
O Gory Baby – Brad Liening
Squeal for Joy – David F. Hoenigman
Pussy Guerilla Face Banana Fuck Nut – RC Miller
Spooky Plan – Drew Kalbach
Vital Signs – Tyson Bley
Mask With Sausage – RC Miller
Death Salad – Brad Liening
Drive-Thru Zoo – Tyson Bley
Necrology – Gary J. Shipley & Kenji Siratori

Made in the USA
Middletown, DE
21 August 2022

71489048R00050